The Totally Awesome 80s TV Trivia Book

THE TOTALLY AWESOME 80S TRIVIA SERIES

Other Books By Michael-Dante Craig

The Totally Awesome 80s Pop Music Trivia Book

The Totally Awesome 80s TV Trivia Book

More Totally Awesome 80s Music Trivia: Volume II

Fast And Furious (novel)

The Totally Awesome 80s TV Trivia Book

Michael-Dante Craig

Writers Club Press
San Jose New York Lincoln Shanghai

The Totally Awesome 80s TV Trivia Book

Writers Club Press
an imprint of iUniverse.com, Inc.

For information address:
iUniverse.com, Inc.
5220 S 16th, Ste. 200
Lincoln, NE 68512
www.iuniverse.com

ISBN: 0-595-18385-9

Printed in the United States of America

For my sister Paula, who helped me survive the 80s with a little help from Bill Cosby, Michael J. Fox and the Golden Girls...

CONTENTS

PREFACE

"*Don't be mean to the television! What has television ever done to you?*"

Homer Simpson

ACKNOWLEDGEMENTS

I must thank the following people for their help, encouragement and support:

Diane Carver Craig, for her love, guidance and support.

My mother, Mary Adams, and my father, Barry Craig.

Jodi Brelsford, for being the best friend anyone could have.

Charles Grosvenor, for being a fountain of information.

Dan Silvia. Jeff Gustafson and everyone at iUniverse, for making my dreams come true.

Special thanks to all of the following: Rhonda Spurr Wilhoite, Miriam Gaeta, Joan Braddy, Marka Mullins, Angela Williams, Vanessa Birch, Tanya Langdon, Claudette D. Pearson, Wendy Williams, Gail Kelly, Viola Pollard, Geneva McDonald, Michael Kennedy, Chad Ambrose, Peggy Golden, Elaine Hoffmire, Neadom Tucker, Sherri Ginn, Leslie Boozer, Margo Holder, Joy Golden, Alfredo Gutierrez, Leticia Puebla, Jason Cromer, Ana Turcios, Maria Corbett, Felix Morales, Joseph Reardon, Mokihana Rausenberg, Tonya Mantooth, Heather Diggett, Christina Kiburz, Chris Mercer, Lee Cooper, Sharon Russell, Wayne Morton, Dot Bailey, Josephine Smith, Sandra Underwood, Amy Ward, Samantha Jackson, Josephine Parker, Michelle Clayton, Marcia Molea, Glenda Padilla, Beverly Adams and Antigone Boatwright.

INTRODUCTION

THE REAL GOLDEN AGE OF TELEVISION: THE 1980S

If you were alive and kicking during the 1980s, then you probably remember watching a great deal of television. Television during the 80s was the great common denominator, bringing together all classes, religions and races. We all laughed together with Bill Cosby and the Golden Girls. We all fell in love with Luke and Laura and Princess Diana and Prince Charles. We felt good when the Duke Boys outwitted Boss Hog, and we all shed tears in unison when the Space Shuttle Challenger exploded before our very eyes.

Television also crossed all geographical and cultural barriers during the 80s. Teenagers in Paris dressed up like "The Fonz"; the British sat down to tea with the cast of *Cheers*; and the Japanese both admired and despised sly J.R. Ewing, along with the rest of the world. For the first time, the Russians could watch American television programs that were not considered to be capitalist propaganda by the Soviet government. News traveled the globe at an amazingly fast pace, making the world seem like a much smaller place in which to live.

If you were a child growing up during the 80s, as I was, then television must have seemed to be an endlessly entertaining fantasyland, filled with amazing stories and characters. The Smurfs taught children how to treat and how not to treat one another. We learned about health and how to take care of our bodies from Mr. Slim Goodbody, whose insides were on his outside. A furry creature from outer space named Alf made us laugh, and Pee-Wee Herman...well, Pee-Wee taught children everywhere that being different was perfectly fine.

The purpose of this book is to test how much useless knowledge you have stored in your brain over the past several decades. This is the perfect game for you to play at your next party, gathering or class reunion. Just imagine how impressed your friends and colleagues will be when they realize just how much time you spent sitting in front of the television during the 80s, the most totally awesome decade of all time!

Who said that television never taught you anything?

Michael-Dante Craig
Cuernavaca, Mexico

PART I:

The Totally Awesome 80s Tv Trivia Challenge

SEE HOW MUCH USELESS TRIVIA FROM THE 80S YOU'VE STORED IN YOUR BRAIN:

1) What did the initials *Alf* stand for?

2) In what state did the *Newhart* show take place?

3) What was the name of Suzanne Somers goofy syndicated sitcom in the 80s?

4) What was the name of the "foundation" that *MacGyver* worked for?

5) What was the name of the android on *Star Trek: The Next Generation?*

6)   What award-winning drama about the Vietnam War starred Dana Delaney and Chloe Webb?

7)   Who was the host of the resurrected version of *The Newlywed Game* in the early 80s?

8)   *Knot's Landing* was a spin-off from what popular night-time soap opera?

9)   What talk show host had his nose broken when a fight among skin-heads erupted on the set of his show?

10)   What sitcom featured Jane Curtin and Susan St. James as New York City divorcees that move in together, along with their children?

11)   *The Simpsons* began as one-minute vignettes on what Fox television show?

12) *TV Guide* caused a furor in 1988 when they placed whose head on the body of Ann-Margaret on its cover?

13) What was the name of the murdered teenaged girl on the bizarre drama *Twin Peaks*?

14) What Australian singer was the original host of the 80s musical variety show *Solid Gold*?

15) What popular show featured the suavely dressed detectives of Crockett and Tubbs?

16) What was the name of Roscoe P. Coltrane's beloved dog on *The Dukes of Hazzard*?

17) On what sitcom did Tom Hanks star as a guy who, along with his friend, dressed up as women to live in a rent controlled, female only apartment complex?

18) What college did Cosby kid Denise attend?

19) Name the wicked wizard that tormented *The Smurfs?*

20) What heartthrob actor was accidentally killed by a stunt gun on the set of the drama *Cover Up* which co-starred Jennifer O'Neal?

21) What was the name of the school that the girls attended on *The Facts of Life?*

22) Before *Friends*, Courteney Cox-Arquette starred on what "oddball" series?

23) What was the name of the detective agency owned by Maddie Hayes on *Moonlighting?*

24) What sort of business did Blake Carrington own on *Dynasty?*

25) Who was the actor that portrayed Ricky Schroeder's buddy on *Silver Spoons* that later went on to star in Michael Jackson's Pepsi commercial?

26) What position did Sam Malone (Ted Danson) play for the Boston Red Sox before buying the bar on *Cheers*?

27) Was the name of Bo and Luke Duke's car on *The Dukes of Hazzard*?

28) What was the name of the bully that tormented Arnold on *Diff'rent Strokes*?

29) What was the name of the elderly lady gossip on *227*?

30) What sort of business did George Jefferson own on *The Jefferson*?

31) What real-life married couple starred on the quintessential 80's drama *thirtysomething*?

32) What was the name of the nursing home where Sofia lived before it burned down on *The Golden Girls*?

33) Which talk show host is known for her trademark red framed eyeglasses?

34) Who was Judge Wapner's bailiff on *The People's Court*?

35) What was the name of the Bundy's dog on *Married With Children*?

36) What blonde news anchor replaced the ever-popular Jane Pauley on *The Today Show* in 1989?

37) Who shot J.R.?

38) Where did Jessica Fletcher live on *Murder, She Wrote*?

39) What "velvet voiced" crooner did Judge Harry Stone admire on *Night Court?*

40) What educational show for kids featured the investigative skills of the Bloodhound Gang?

41) What famed school was the setting for the TV version of *Fame?*

42) What game show featured the dreaded "Whammies"?

43) On what street did Dan and Roseanne Connor live on *Roseanne?*

44) What show starred Joseph Bologna as a single millionaire that adopts a large group of orphaned girls and turns them into a singing group?

45) What was the name of the Tanners nosy neighbor on *Alf?*

46) What Rolling Stone song was used in the opening of *Tour of Duty*?

47) What was the name of the character with Downs Syndrome on *Life Goes On*?

48) Who was Murphy's house painter on *Murphy Brown*?

49) On *Falcon Crest*, what was the family business?

50) Where did the ladies work on *Alice*?

51) What was the name of Norm's never-seen wife on *Cheers*?

52) What were the names of Higgins' Dobermans on *Magnum P.I.?*

53) On the early episodes of *The Facts of Life*, what was the character of Tootie seldom seen without?

54) What was the name of Bill Bixby's character before he transformed into *The Incredible Hulk?*

55) Who was hired as the Aunt on *The Hogan Family* after Valerie Harper was fired during a contract dispute?

56) What was the first name of J.R. Ewing's personal secretary on *Dallas?*

57) What did Saundra and Eldin name their twins on *The Cosby Show?*

58) What 80s pop star appeared as himself on an episode of *The A Team?*

59) What phrase had to be spoken on *You Can't Do That on Television* to cause the person to have green slime to be dumped on their heads?

60) What was the name of the blue Genie on *Pee-Wee's Playhouse?*

61) What was the name of Michael Knight's car on *Knight Rider?*

62) Where did *Roseanne* and her sister Jackie work before getting laid off?

63) What type of doctor was Dr. Harry Weston (played by Richard Mulligan) on *Empty Nest?*

64) What was Dorothy's profession on *The Golden Girls?*

65) What was the name of the Valley Girl character (played to perfection by Tracy Nelson) on *Square Pegs?*

66) In the last season of *Laverne and Shirley,* where did the girls live after leaving Milwaukee?

67) What star of *LA Law* was voted "Sexiest Man Alive" by *People* magazine on its cover in 1989?

68) What two shows did Heather Locklear appear on simultaneously during the early 80s?

69) In what show did Lee Majors portray an aging stunt man?

70) What southern city was the setting for *Designing Women*?

71) What drama starred Deidre Hall as a single mother raising her son and daughter with the help of crusty curmudgeon Wilford Brimley?

72) What was the name of the dippy secretary on *Moonlighting*?

73) After John Schneider and Tom Wopat left *The Dukes of Hazzard,* what character was brought in as a less-than-stellar replacement?

74) What was the last name of the family that adopted Emmanuel Lewis' character on *Webster*?

75) Who was the smart alec waitress on *What's Happening Now?*

76) What was the name of Sherman Helmsley character on *Amen?*

77) What popular catch phrase did Clara Peller make famous in commercials for Wendy's hamburgers?

78) What famous mini-series featured Richard Chamberlain as Father Ralph and his forbidden love affair with Meghan Cleary?

79) What critically acclaimed Canadian teen drama featured a young Neve Campbell?

80) What was the name of the inn owned by Dick Louden on *Newhart?*

81) What sitcom starred Greg Evigan and Paul Reiser as two single guys raising a teenaged girl?

82) What sitcom starring Howard Hesseman also showcased the diverse talents of Robin Givens?

83) What was the name of the St. Bernard on *Empty Nest?*

84) What show did Murphy anchor on *Murphy Brown?*

85) What town was the setting for *In the Heat of the Night?*

86) What show featured Robert Guillame as a sarcastic butler working in the Governor's mansion?

87) What was the nickname of the extremely tall bailiff on *Night Court?*

88) Who was the head mistress of the girl's school on *The Facts of Life?*

89) On *BJ and the Bear,* what type of animal was Bear?

90) Name all five of the Cosby kids in chronological order, oldest to youngest.

91) What was the name of Alex's best friend on *Family Ties*?

92) Who was the first woman hired to co-anchor *60 Minutes*?

93) What was the name of the Tanner family cat that *Alf* always wanted to eat?

94) What was the name of Kirstie Alley's character on *Cheers*?

95) What show starred Jon-Eric Hexum as time travelling rapscallion Phineas Boggs?

96) Who starred as TV's *Punky Brewster*?

97) What acclaimed Broadway actress portrayed the frazzled Mom on *Life Goes On*?

98) Who was Arnie Becker's dedicated personal secretary on *LA Law*?

99) What prime time soap starred Morgan Fairchild, John Beck and Stella Stevens?

100) Where did Al Bundy work on *Married With Children*?

101) What type of car did *Starsky & Hutch* drive?

102) What was Julia and Suzanne's last name on *Designing Women*?

103) What soap opera was cancelled in 1986 after a record breaking thirty-five year run?

104) What Civil War mini-series was based on a John Jake's novel and starred Patrick Swayzee and Kiristie Alley?

105) What was the actual name of the hospital on *St. Elsewhere*?

106) The last episode of what popular, long running show was the most watched show of all time when it aired in 1983?

107) What comedic actor popularized the characters of Gumby and Buckwheat on *Saturday Night Live*?

108) What city was the setting for *Full House*?

109) What was *Matlock's* first name?

110) What two shows did Bob Saget appear on during the 80s?

111) What was the name of the character portrayed by Jim Varney in countless television commercials?

112) What was the name of *Buck Rogers'* robotic sidekick?

113) Who played the sarcastic cab dispatcher on *Taxi?*

114) What Mid-Western town was the setting of *Little House on the Prairie?*

115) Who was the bartender on *The Love Boat?*

116) What was the name of Howard Hesseman's DJ character on *WKRP in Cincinnati?*

117) What was Florence Jean Castleberry's catch phrase on *Alice?*

118) What was the Lieutenant's advice to his officers every day after roll call on *Hill Street Blues*?

119) What series starred Dabney Coleman as a neurotic sports caster for a local television station?

120) What daytime drama featured the super-couple of Jenny and Greg?

121) Which male talk show host once appeared on his show wearing a full-length skirt?

122) Who replaced Tom Brokaw as co-anchor on *The Today Show*?

123) Who was the upbeat next door neighbor of *The Hogan Family*?

124) What did the initials in *Chips* represent?

125) What long-running dance show for teens hosted by Dick Clark was cancelled in 1989?

126) What mini-series starring Marc Singer and Robert Englund was about the earth being invaded by aliens in search of a new food supply: humans?

127) What was the name of the dog on *Hart to Hart?*

128) What western city was the setting of the prime time sudser *Dynasty?*

129) What was the nickname that Rudy gave her "boyfriend" on *The Cosby Show?*

130) Who starred as the title character on *The Days and Nights of Molly Dodd?*

131) Who was the British millionaire that Kirstie Alley's character was madly in love with on *Cheers?*

132) What Academy-Award winning actress portrayed Angela Channing on *Falcon Crest*?

133) What show had cameo appearances by Sheena Easton, Phil Collins and Melanie Griffith?

134) What highly acclaimed British daytime drama debuted on PBS in the mid-80s?

135) What did they call Gregory Harrison's character on *Trapper John, M.D.*?

136) What was the failed sequel to *M*A*S*H* called?

137) What sweeping WWII epic mini-series was based on a Herman Wouk best-selling novel?

138) What did *Mr. Belvedere* always do at the end of each show?

139) What show starred Bruce Boxleitner and Kate Jackson as secret agents?

140) For what television drama did both Sharon Gless and Tyne Daly win Emmy awards?

141) Where did the detectives on *21 Jump Street* do their undercover work?

142) *Gimme A Break* showcased the talents of what Tony-Award winning actress?

143) What was the name of the girl that Kevin Arnold loved on *The Wonder Years*?

144) What two legends hosted *TV's Bloopers and Practical Jokes*?

145) What was the name of the moonshine producing elderly ladies on *The Waltons*?

146) What actor played Booker, Roseanne and Jackie's boss, on *Roseanne*?

147) On what soap opera did Meg Ryan appear as Betsy Andropolous?

148) What was the last name of the family on *Growing Pains*?

149) Who is Cassandra Petersen's alter ego?

150) Who was the dippy neighbor played by JM J. Bullock on *Too Close for Comfort*?

151) What were the first names of the brothers on *Simon and Simon*?

152) On whose estate did *Magnum P.I.* live?

153) What "corn pone" comedy featured the talents of Buck Owens, Grandpa Jones and Lulu?

154) Who sang the notes on *Name That Tune?*

155) What did Robin Leach say at the end of every episode of *Lifestyles of the Rich and Famous?*

156) What short-lived comedy did Delta Burke and Dixie Carter star on together before *Designing Women?*

157) What real-life married couple acted together on *LA Law?*

158) What actress replaced Suzanne Somers when she was fired from *Three's Company?*

159 Who played the character of Jenna Wade on *Dallas?*

160) What sci-fi series starred Lorne Green and Dirk Benedict?

161) What did Arsenio Hall call the audience members seated behind the house band on his talk show?

162) What was the name of Bronson Pinchot's character on *Perfect Strangers*?

163) Who usually filled in for Johnny Carson on *The Tonight Show* before getting her own late night talk show on the Fox network, igniting a feud with the talk show titan?

164) What ventriloquist/puppet team was prominently featured on *Solid Gold*?

165) Who was the wardrobe designer for *Dynasty?*

166) What series starred Stephanie Beacham as a nun caring for a group of orphans?

167) What show was about a group of cocktail waitresses working in a high-rise lounge?

168) What series did Rock Hudson star on with Jack Scalia shortly before his death?

169) What television show would not let Pierce Brosnan out of his contract when he was originally offered the role of James Bond in the late 80s?

170) Who starred as TV's *The Bionic Woman*?

171) What was the name of Shirley's beloved stuffed animal on *Laverne & Shirley*?

172) On *Mork and Mindy*, what was the name of Mork's home planet?

173) Who originally played the character of evil Helena Cassadine on *General Hospital*?

174) What sweeping epic mini-series set in feudal Japan starred Richard Chamberlain and was based on a popular novel by James Clavel?

175) Who was the host of *This Old House* during the 80s?

176) Which Dana Carvey character from *Saturday Night Live* popularized the catch phrases "Well, isn't that special" and "Was it SATAN, perhaps"?

177) What show starring Erin Moran and Scott Baio was a spin-off from *Happy Days*?

178) What beautiful news anchorwoman was killed in a tragic car accident in 1982?

179) What crime drama starred acclaimed English actor Edward Woodward?

180) What shocking disaster was broadcast on live television in February, 1986?

181) What real life show did Cathy Lee Crosby, Fran Tarkington and John Davidson host?

182) What 70s love anthology series became popular again in the 80s when it went into syndication?

183) Who was the affable host of *The Love Connection* and *Scrabble*?

184) What soap opera featured the super couple Cruz and Eden?

185) Who played no-nonsense bailiff Roz on *Night Court*?

186) What show was revered comic Andy Kaufman a cast member before his untimely death?

187) What acclaimed (but short-lived) drama starred Jason Robards as the cantankerous head of a dysfunctional American family?

188) What show had Simon McCorkindale transforming into a dangerous, feral creature?

189) What was the name of Craig T. Nelson's character on *Coach*?

190) Who became the landlord after the Roper's left *Three's Company*?

191) Who is Homer Simpson's nefarious boss at the nuclear power plant on *The Simpsons*?

192) What show starred Pam Dawber and Rebecca Schaefer, who was later killed by an obsessed fan?

193) What cop drama was former football star Fred Dryer's starring vehicle?

194) What former Mr. Universe played *The Incredible Hulk*?

195) Who taught kids about anatomy and health by wearing a suit displaying all the body organs and muscles?

196) What primetime news anchor walked off the set of a nightly news program in protest after the news was pre-empted by a tennis match?

197) What show starred a high-tech helicopter along with Jan-Michael Vincent?

198) What horror anthology series did the Cryptkeeper host?

199) Who did Charlie Gibson replace on *Good Morning, America*?

200) Who was Fonzi's biker chick girlfriend on *Happy Days*?

201) What pint-sized actor portrayed TV's *Webster*?

202) What rotund actor starred as the Fat Man on *Jake and the Fat Man*?

203) Who started the program *America's Most Wanted* after the abduction and murder of his son, Adam?

204) Who was the voice of Charlie on *Charlie's Angels*?

205) Who was the host of *Star Search*?

206) Who hosted the resurrected version of *The Hollywood Squares* in the 80s?

207) What was the first name of Jasmine Guy's spoiled rich girl character on *A Different World*?

208) What television show featured a pig-tailed, freckle-faced robot girl?

209) What new wave band sang the theme song to *Square Pegs*?

210) What character did Mr. T play on *The A Team*?

211) What did Oprah pull onto the stage in a little red wagon after she lost an impressive amount of weight?

212) Who played Jennifer the secretary on *WKRP in Cincinnati?*

213) What show starred Dan Haggerty as an escaped con hiding out in the beautiful Rocky Mountains?

214) Who were the neighbors of the Weston's on *Empty Nest?*

215) What show featured the nerdy character Screech played by nerdy actor Dustin Diamond?

216) What super couple's wedding drew a record breaking number of soap viewers in 1982?

217) What series starred Tom Bosley as a mystery-solving priest?

218) What was the last name of Tony Danza's character on *Who's the Boss?*

219) Who was the suave host of *Soul Train* in the 70s and 80s?

220) What show starred Lance Kerwin as an angst-ridden teenager?

221) Who was the captain of the Starship Enterprise on *Star Trek: The Next Generation*?

222) Who starred as Buddy on *Family*?

223) What show starred Peter Barton as an alien teen with telekinetic powers?

224) What are Bob Barker's lovely assistants known as on *The Price is Right*?

225) What did you want to "avoid" in the Domino's Pizza commercials?

226) Who hosted TV's *American Top 10*?

227) What series starred Scott Bakula as a time-travelling, identity switching man?

228) Who played Valene Ewing on *Knot's Landing*?

229) What was the name of the handyman on *One Day at a Time*?

230) What dance contest did Denny Terrio host?

231) What actress replaced Farrah Fawcett when she left *Charlie's Angels*?

232) Name all four of the *Teenaged Mutant Ninja Turtles*:

233) What British comedy featured the character Neil and his squatter friends?

234) Who was the original host of *Unsolved Mysteries*?

235) What show was about a family plunged into a land inhabited by the Sleestack and dinosaurs after the "greatest earthquake ever known"?

236) What animated band made raisins a popular treat in the late 80s?

237) Farrah Fawcett portrayed an abused wife in what successful television movie?

238) What show starred Linda Hamilton as Catherine Chandler and her forbidden love for "Vincent"?

239) What stuttering, computerized character appeared in commercials for New Coke and even had his own television show?

240) What was the name of the only female *Smurf*?

241) What show starred Judd Hirsch as a man coping with divorce by attending meetings with other divorcees?

242) By what name is Bob Keenan better known?

243) What popular actress/comedienne/talk show hostess got her big break by winning on *Star Search*?

244) What was the name of the youngest son (played by Adam Rich) on *Eight is Enough*?

245) What did the old man always say at the end of the commercials for Bartles & James' wine coolers?

246) What "red neck" billionaire is the founder of the CNN cable network?

247) What award-winning daytime drama was centered around a large, working class, Irish-American family living in New York City?

248) What mid-Western city was the setting for *Family Ties*?

249) What sitcom starred Gerald McRaney as a military family man?

250) Who was the head of NBC that was credited with making the Peacock Network Number One in the ratings in the early 80s?

251) What was the name of Alan Thicke's failed late night talk show?

252) Vanna White starred as a goddess in what tacky movie of the week?

253) What game show hosted by Ken Ober debuted on MTV in 1987?

254) What is the name of the town where *The Simpsons'* live?

255) What gritty detective series starred Stacy Keach in the mid-80s?

256) Who was the twin sister of *He-Man?*

257) What was host Richard Dawson famous for doing to his female contestants on *Family Feud?*

258) Who starred as Mama on *Mama's Family*?

259) What league did the *Super Friends* belong to on the cartoon series?

260) What actor portrayed teen doctor *Doogie Howser, M.D.*?

261) What controversial mini-series was about the United States being invaded and conquered by the Soviet Union, and drew protests from the Russian government?

262) Who starred as the grown-up daughter of witch Samantha Stevens on the spin-off series of *Bewitched, Tabitha*?

263) Who were the original hosts of *Sneak Previews*?

264) What show starring Burt Reynolds and Elizabeth Ashley focused on the eccentric residents of a small southern town?

265) What did Barbara Walters always say at the end of each broadcast of *20/20*?

266) Who originally hosted *A Current Affair*?

267) What yearly television staple showcased stars performing death-defying acts?

268) What "angelic" actress starred in the television mini-series *A Woman Named Jackie*, about the life of Jackie Kennedy Onassis?

269) What pint-sized sex therapist opened up America's eyes to sex with her television talk show?

270) What mega-producer was responsible for the hit shows *The Love Boat*, *Charlie's Angels* and *Dynasty*?

271) What was the name of Marcy's second husband on *Married With Children*?

272) What best-selling novelist created the hit show *Hart to Hart*?

273) What mystery based soap opera ended its thirty year plus run in 1984?

274) What syndicated, half-hour entertainment news program debuted in 1981?

275) In what city did the Connor family reside on *Roseanne*?

276) Name three of the five original MTV veejays:

277) What debonair Latin actor hawked Chrysler Cordoba's with their seats made of "rich Corinthian leather" in TV ads?

278) What was the name of *Alf's* home planet?

279) What show starred Ann Jillian as the ghost of a famous actress?

280) What horror mini-series, based on a Stephen King novel, was about an evil clown named Pennywise?

281) What talk show host opened Al Capone's secret vault in Chicago, live on television, with disappointing results?

282) What educational PBS series did Levar Burton begin hosting in the early 80s?

283) What was the name of the Jolly Green Giant's little friend?

284) What actress replaced Pamela Sue Martin (with a British accent) in the role of Fallon on *Dynasty*?

285) Who were *Laverne & Shirley's* annoying neighbors?

286) What did Hannibal Smith always say at the end of each episode of *The A Team*?

287) What singer/actress starred on *Friday the 13th: The Series*?

288) Who helped hide *The Littles* on the cartoon series?

289) Where did *Mork and Mindy* live (on Earth)?

290) Who starred as TV's Sheriff Lobo?

291) What mini-series starred Lindsay Wagner and was based on a popular Judith Krantz bestseller?

292) What was the occupation of Alan Thicke's character on *Growing Pains*?

293) What pop star played the role of Charlene, Willis' girlfriend, on *Diff'rent Strokes*?

294) *Nightline*, hosted by Ted Koppel, debuted during what political crisis in 1980?

295) What talk show host played the role of Nurse Holly on *China Beach*?

296) What was the name of Lee Major's character on *The Six Million Dollar Man?*

297) What was the name of Woody's hometown on *Cheers?*

298) What was the name of *Punky Brewster's* dog?

299) What soap became the top rated daytime drama in 1987, and has remained in that spot every year since?

300) What sort of company did Ann Romano work for on *One Day at a Time?*

301) What mantra-like slogan did MTV use to snare viewers in the early 80s?

302) What HBO comedy show lampooned television network news?

303) What was the name of the religious talk show founded by Pat Robertson?

304) Who starred as Charles on *Charles in Charge?*

305) Who played the maid Florence on *The Jeffersons?*

306) What was the name of *Grizzly Adams'* Indian blood brother?

307 What actress played Michael J. Fox's love interest on *Family Ties,* and later became the actor's real life wife?

308) What was the name of Suzanne's pet pig on *Designing Women?*

309) Who hosted the *$25,000 Pyramid*?

310) Who hosted *Rescue 911*?

311) Fonzi's leather jacket and Archie Bunker's recliner are exhibited in the Pop Culture gallery at what museum?

312) What was the name of Dorothy's cross dressing brother on *The Golden Girls*?

313) What "gothic" soap opera about vampire Barnabus Collins experienced newfound popularity in syndication on PBS?

314) What Oscar winning actress portrayed Guinan, the wise proprietress of 10 Forward on *Star Trek: The Next Generation*?

315) What former football great starred at TV's *Father Murphy*?

316) What was the name of *Jonny Quest's* turban wearing friend?

317) Who was J.R. and Sue Ellen's son on *Dallas*?

318) What was the name of the van used by *Scooby-Doo* and his friends?

319) What spin-off from *21 Jump Street* starred Richard Grieco?

320) What made-for-TV movie starring Jason Robards and Steve Guttenberg was about a nuclear war and its horrific aftermath?

321) What country and western artist sang the theme song to *The Dukes of Hazzard*?

322) What was the name of *The Bionic Woman*?

323) Who starred as Buck in *Buck Rogers in the 25th Century*?

324) What was the name of Laura Ingles archenemy on *Little House on the Prairie*?

325) What was Laverne's favorite drink on *Laverne & Shirley*?

326) Where did Fonzi live on *Happy Days*?

327) What comedic actor narrated *The Wonder Years*?

328) Who played the trombone and lead the house band on *The Tonight Show* with Johnny Carson?

329) Who was the host on *The New Tic-Tac-Dough*?

330) What rotund announcer wore brightly colored suits and shouted "Come on down!" on *The Price is Right*?

331) What town did the family live in on *Mama's Family*?

332) What was the name of the inept maid played by Julia Duffy on *Newhart*?

333) What television series starring Barbara Eden was based on a popular motion picture and hit song?

334) What comedy show starred Fred Williard opposite Krofft puppet facsimiles of Hollywood celebrities and political figures?

335) Name all of Scooby-Doo's cohorts.

336) What was the name of the town in the Ozarks where Charlene grew up on *Designing Women?*

337) Who was the original host of *Matchgame?*

338) Which resort island was the setting of *Wings?*

339) What classic 60s song was used in the opening of the gritty drama *Crime Story* starring Dennis Farina?

340) What type of alien was Lt. Worf on *Star Trek: The Next Generation*?

341) What town was the setting of *Picket Fences*?

342) What show starred Robert Blake as an unlikely priest?

343) Who portrayed sexy millionaire *Matt Houston*?

344) What game show for kids was broadcast on Nickelodeon and hosted by Marc Summers?

345) What prime time soap starred Connie Selleca and James Brolin as the proprietors of a posh San Francisco establishment?

346) What talk show hostess/singer was featured in commercials for "Jean Nate" body splash in the early 80s?

347) What macho actor starred as *B.L. Stryker?*

348) What actor portrayed Dan Connor's father on *Roseanne?*

349) Who was the original host of the game show *Win, Lose, or Draw!* ?

350) What was Mork's standard greeting on *Mork and Mindy?*

351) Who was *Benson*'s dour arch-nemesis?

352) What actor played the character of Jodie Dallas on the satire *Soap,* television's first gay character?

353) What famed producer created the shows *All in the Family, Maude* and *The Jeffersons?*

354) What Nickelodeon program featured old movies dubbed over with hilarious ad-libs?

355) What educational PBS children's series had Rita Moreno and Morgan Freeman among its cast?

356) What actress played the characters of Roseanne Roseanna Danna and Barbara Wawa on *Saturday Night Live*?

357) What pop star sang the theme song to *The Greatest American Hero*?

358) What show starred Sir John Gielgud as an uptight college professor?

359) What is Mister Rogers first name?

360) What NBC soap was the first daytime drama to be centered around an African American family?

361) What revered actor said "They will sell no wine before its time", in television ads for Paul Mason?

362) What type of "pet" did Sonny keep on his boat on *Miami Vice*?

363) What producer/director was responsible for the bizarre drama *Twin Peaks*?

364) What type of alien was Counselor Troi on *Star Trek: The Next Generation*?

365) Who played "rich bitch" Alexis Colby Carrington on *Dynasty*?

366) What actress appeared as Burt Reynolds wife on *Evening Shade*?

367) Who was Barbara Walters' thrill seeking co-anchor on *20/20*?

368) What actors appeared as *The Hardy Boys*?

369) What alcoholic beverage did Bruce Willis hawk in television ads?

370) What two pop stars sang the theme song to *Family Ties?*

371) In what series did Michael Landon star as an angel, returned to earth to save lost souls?

372) What syndicated musical series was about the "exploits" of a 50s doo-wop band?

373) What rugged actor dared viewers to knock an Eveready battery off his shoulder in television ads?

374) What superstar dog was the mascot for Budweiser beer?

375) What star of the soap opera *The Young and The Restless* scored a number one hit on the Pop charts in 1989 with "Rock On"?

376) What monumental benefit concert for world hunger was broadcast to over two billion people in June, 1985?

377) Who was the Drummond family's original house keeper/nanny on *Diff'rent Strokes?*

378) What 80s anthology series did Steven Spielberg produce?

379) Who was J.R. and Bobby Ewing's "daddy" on *Dallas?*

380) What type of doctor was Dr. Cliff Huxtable on *The Cosby Show?*

381) What educational show for kids featured Gary Gnu and his segment "No gnus is good gnus"?

382) Who hosted the 80s version of the game show *Classic Concentration?*

383) What was Cliff's occupation on *Cheers?*

384) Who was the young, be-spectacled producer of the news program on *Murphy Brown?*

385) What cable network was promoted as an "MTV for grown-ups"?

386) What superstar wrote and sang the theme song to *American Bandstand?*

387) What delivery company used the world's "fastest talking man" in their television ads?

388) What "pantomime" game show did Tom Kennedy host?

389) What was *Punky Brewster's* actual first name?

390) From what city were the 1988 Summer Olympic Games broadcast?

391) Who interviewed Mike Tyson and Robins Givens on television just days before their separation and subsequent divorce?

392) In commercials for Hertz Rental Car Agency, what disgraced athlete was seen running (and leaping over suitcases) through a busy airport?

393) Finish the name of this 80s comedy/drama: *Hardcastle &* _____.

394) What actors played the long-suffering couple of Mac and Karen on *Knot's Landing*?

395) Who played the Dad on *Eight Is Enough*?

396) What was the name of *Mork and Mindy's* son (played by Jonathon Winters)?

397) What legendary comedienne played daughter Eunice on *Mama's Family*?

398) What Ivy League college was Scott Baio's character accepted to on the final episode of *Charles in Charge*?

399) What did John-Boy aspire to be on *The Waltons*?

400) What famous jingle did McDonald's use to promote Big Mac sandwiches in their television advertisements?

PART II:

THE TOTALLY AWESOME 80S TV TRIVIA
ANSWERS

Now it's time to check how you did.

1) Alien Life Form

2) Vermont

3) *She's the Sheriff*

4) The Phoenix Foundation

5) Data

6) *China Beach*

7)   Bob Eubanks

8)   *Dallas*

9)   Geraldo Rivera

10)   *Kate and Allie*

11)   *The Tracy Ullman Show*

12)   Oprah Winfrey

13)   Laura Palmer

14)   Andy Gibb

15) *Miami Vice*

16) Flash

17) *Bosom Buddies*

18) Hillman College

19) Gargamyl

20) Jon-Eric Hexum

21) Eastland Girl's Academy

22) *Misfits of Science*

23) Blue Moon Detective Agency

24) Carrington Oil

25) Alfonso Ribeiro

26) Pitcher

27) General Lee

28) The Gooch

29) Pearl

30) Dry cleaning

31) Ken Olin and Patricia Wettig

32) Shady Pines

33) Sally Jessy-Raphael

34) Rusty

35) Buck

36) Deborah Norville

37) Kristin Shepard

38) Cabot Cove, Maine

39) Mel Torme

40) *3-2-1 Contact*

41) New York Academy of Performing Arts

42) *Press Your Luck*

43) The corner of 3rd Avenue and Delaware Street

44) *Rags To Riches*

45) *Mrs. Ochmonik*

46) "Paint It Black"

47) Corky

48) Eldin

49) A winery

50) Mel's Diner

51) Vera

52) Zeus and Apollo

53) Her roller skates

54) Dr. David Banner

55) Sandy Duncan

56) Sly

57) Nelson and Winnie

58) Boy George

59) "I don't know"

60) Jambi

61) KITT

62) Wellman plastic factory

63) A pediatrician

64) Substitute teacher

65) Jennifer de Nuccio

66) Hollywood, California

67) Harry Hamlin

68) *Dynasty* and *TJ Hooker*

69) *The Fall Guy*

70) Atlanta, Georgia

71) *Our House*

72) Ms. Depesto

73) Cousin Coy

74) Papadopolous

75) Shirley

76) Deacon Earnest Fry

77) "Where's the beef?"

78) *The Thorn Birds*

79) *Degrassi Junior High*

80) The Stratford Inn

81) *My Two Dads*

82) *Head of the Class*

83) Dreyfuss

84) *FYI*

85) Sparta

86) *Benson*

87) Bull

88) Mrs. Garrett

89) Chimpanzee

90) Saundra, Denise, Theo, Vanessa, Ruby

91) Skippy

92) Diane Sawyer

93) Lucky

94) Rebecca Howell

95) *Voyagers*

96) Soleil-Moon Frye

97) Patty Lupone

98) Roxanne

99) *Flamingo Road*

100) A shoe store

101) '75 Ford Torino

102) Sugabaker

103) Search for Tomorrow

104) North and South

105) St. Elegius

106) M*A*S*H

107) Eddie Murphy

108) San Francisco

109) Benjamin

110) Full House, America's Funniest Home Videos

111) Ernest P. Worrell

112) Twiki

113) Danny DeVito

114) Walnut Grove, Minnesota

115) Isaac

116) Johnny Fever

117) "Kiss My Grits."

118) "You guys be careful out there, okay?"

119) Buffalo Bill

120) All My Children

121) Phil Donahue

122) Bryant Gumbel

123) Mrs. Poole

124) California Highway Patrol

125) American Bandstand

126) V

127) Freeway

128) Denver, Colorado

129) "Bud"

130) Blair Brown

131) Robin Colcord

132) Jane Wyman

133) Miami Vice

134) The East Enders

135) Gonzo

136) *After M*A*S*H*

137) *The Winds of War, War and Remembrance*

138) Wrote in his journal

139) *Scarecrow and Mrs. King*

140) *Cagney & Lacey*

141) High school

142) Nell Carter

143) Winnie

144) Dick Clark and Ed McMahon

145) The Baldwin sisters

146) George Clooney

147) As the World Turns

148) The Seavers

149) Elvira, Mistress of the Dark

150) Monroe

151) Rick and A.J.

152) Robin Masters

153) Hee Haw!

154) Kathie Lee Gifford

155) "Champagne wishes and caviar dreams…"

156) Filthy Rich

157) Michael Tucker and Jill Eikenberry

158) Priscilla Barnes

159) Priscilla Presley

160) Battlestar Gallactica

161) The Dog Pound

162) Balki Bartokomous

163) Joan Rivers

164) Wayland Flowers and Madame

165) Nolan Miller

166) Sister Kate

167) It's a Living

168) The Devlin Connection

169) Remington Steel

170) Lindsay Wagner

171) Boo-Boo Kitty

172) Ork

173) Elizabeth Taylor

174) Shogun

175) Bob Vila

176) The Church Lady

177) *Joani Loves Chachi*

178) Jessica Savitch

179) *The Equalizer*

180) The Space Shuttle Challenger disaster

181) *That's Incredible*

182) *Love: American Style*

183) Chuck Woolery

184) Santa Barbara

185) Marsha Warfield

186) Taxi

187) A Year in the Life

188) Manimal

189) Hayden Fox

190) Mr. Farley

191) Mr. Burns

192) My Sister Sam

193) Hunter

194) Lou Ferigno

195) Mr. Slim Goodbody

196) Dan Rather

197) Airwolf

198) Tales from the Crypt

199) Dave Hartman

200) Pinky Toscadero

201) Emmanuel Lewis

202) William Conrad

203) John Walsh

204) John Forsythe

205) Ed McMahon

206) John Davidson

207) Whitley

208) Small Wonder

209) The Waitresses

210) B.A. Baracus

211) 67 pounds of beef fat

212) Lonnie Anderson

213) The Life and Times of Grizzly Adams

214) The cast of *The Golden Girls*

215) Saved by the Bell

216) Luke and Laura

217) Father Dowling Mysteries

218) Micelli

219) Don Cornelius

220) James at Fifteen

221) Captain Jean-Luc Picard

222) Kristy McNichol

223) The Powers of Matthew Star

224) Barker's Beauties

225) The Noid

226) Casey Kasem

227) Quantum Leap

228) Joan Van Ark

229) Schroeder

230) Dance Fever

231) Cheryl Ladd

232) Michaelangelo, Donnatello, Raphael, Leonardo

233) *The Young Ones*

234) Carl Malden

235) *The Land of the Lost*

236) The California Raisins

237) *The Burning Bed*

238) *Beauty and the Beast*

239) Max Headroom

240) Smurfette

241) Dear John

242) Captain Kangaroo

243) Rosie O'Donnell

244) Nicholas Bradford

245) "And we thank you for your support."

246) Ted Turner

247) *Ryan's Hope*

248) Columbus, Ohio

249) *Major Dad*

250) Brandon Tartikoff

251) *In the Thicke of the Night*

252) *Venus: Goddess of Love*

253) *Remote Control*

254) Springfield

255) Mike Hammer

256) She-Ra

257) Kissing each female contestant

258) Vicky Lawrence

259) The Justice League of America

260) Neil Patrick Harris

261) Amerika

262) Lisa Hartman (Black)

263) Siskel and Ebert

264) *Evening Shade*

265) "We'll be in touch, so you be in touch."

266) Maury Povich

267) *The Circus of the Stars*

268) Roma Downey

269) Dr. Ruth Westheimer

270) Aaron Spelling

271) Jefferson Darcy

272) Sidney Sheldon

273) *The Edge of Night*

274) *Entertainment Tonight*

275) Lanford, Illinois

276) Martha Quinn, J.J. Jackson, Nina Blackwood, Alan Hunter, Mark Goodman

277) Ricardo Montalban

278) Melmac

279) Jennifer Slept Here

280) Stephen King's It

281) Geraldo Rivera

282) Reading Rainbow

283) Sprout

284) Emma Samms

285) Lenny and Squiggy

286) "I love it when a plan comes together."

287) Robey

288) Henry Big

289) Boulder, Colorado

290) Claude Akins

291) Scruples

292) Psychiatrist

293) Janet Jackson

294) Iranian hostage crisis

295) Ricki Lake

296) Steve Austin

297) Hanover, Indiana

298) Brandon

299) *The Young and the Restless*

300) Advertising company

301) "I want my MTV!"

302) *Not Necessarily the News*

303) *The 700 Club*

304) Scott Baio

305) Marla Gibbs

306) Nakuma

307) Tracey Pollan

308) Noel

309) Dick Clark

310) William Shatner

311) The Smithsonian

312) Phil

313) *Dark Shadows*

314) Whoopi Goldberg

315) Merlin Olsen

316) Hadji

317) John Ross

318) The Mystery Machine

319) *Booker*

320) *The Day After*

321) Waylon Jennings

322) Jamie Sommers

323) Gil Gerard

324) Nellie Olson

325) Pepsi and milk

326) Above the Cunningham's garage

327) Daniel Stern

328) Doc Severinsen

329) Wink Martindale

330) Rod Roddy

331) Raytown

332) Stephanie

333) *Harper Valley, PTA*

334) *DC Follies*

335) Shaggy, Daphne, Fred, Velma

336) Poplar Bluff, Missouri

337) Gene Rayburn

338) Nantucket

339) "Runaway" by Del Shannon

340) half human, half Klingon

341) Rome, Wisconsin

342) *Helltown*

343) Lee Horsley

344) *Double Dare*

345) *Hotel*

346) Kathie Lee Gifford

347) Burt Reynolds

348) Ned Beatty

349) Bert Convy

350) "Nanu Nanu"

351) Miss Kraus

352) Billy Crystal

353) Norman Lear

354) *Mad Movies with the LA Connection*

355) *The Electric Company*

356) Gilda Radner

357) Joey Scarbury

358) *The Paper Chase*

359) Fred

360) *Generations*

361) Orson Wells

362) An alligator

363) David Lynch

364) Betazoid

365) Joan Collins

366) Marilu Henner

367) Hugh Downs

368) Shaun Cassidy, Parker Stevenson

369) Seagram's Golden Wine Coolers

370) Johnny Mathis and Deniece Williams

371) *Highway to Heaven*

372) *Sha-Na-Na*

373) Robert Conrad

374) Spuds MacKenzie

375) Michael Damian

376) Live Aid Benefit Concert

377) Mrs. Garrett

378) *Amazing Stories*

379) Jock Ewing

380) Ob/gyn

381) *The Great Space Coaster*

382) Alex Trebek

383) Postal carrier

384) Miles Silverberg

385) VH1

386) Barry Mannilow

387) Federal Express

388) *Body Language*

389) Penelope

390) Seoul, South Korea

391) Barbara Walters

392) O.J. Simpson

393) McCormick

394) Michelle Lee and Kevin Dobson

395) Dick Van Patten

396) Mearth

397) Carol Burnette

398) Princeton

399) A writer and journalist

400) "Two all beef patties, special sauce, lettuce, cheese, pickle, onion on a sesame seed bun…"

The End

ABOUT THE AUTHOR

Michael-Dante Craig is the author of the best selling *Totally Awesome 80s Trivia Series*. A native of Kentucky, he currently divides his time between homes in Charleston, South Carolina, and Cuernavaca, Mexico. He is currently working on his first novel, as well as another book in the trivia series. He welcomes e-mails with your thoughts and comments at Popupvid28@aol.com.

Notes

For more information about Michael-Dante Craig and his books, please visit his web site at:

http://hometown.aol.com/popupvid28/index.html

Made in the USA
San Bernardino, CA
14 May 2014